Sew Beautifully

50 Quick and Easy Applique Designs Book for Crafting Stunning Creations

Frederick T Raj

THIS BOOK BELONGS TO
The Library of

....

....

I can't tell you how grateful I am that you decided to read my book. My most heartfelt thanks that you took time out of your life to choose my work and I hope you find benefit within these pages.

There are so many books available today that offer similar content so that makes it even more humbling that you decided to buying mine.

Tell me what you thought! I am eager to hear your opinion and ideas on what you read as are others who are looking for a good book to buy. Leave a review on Amazon.com so others can benefit from your wisdom!

With much thanks.

Table of Contents

SUMMARY

Introduction to Appliqué:

Appliqué is a decorative technique that involves attaching fabric pieces onto a larger fabric surface to create a design or pattern. It is a popular method used in various crafts, such as quilting, sewing, and embroidery. This technique allows for endless possibilities in creating unique and personalized designs on fabric.

The history of appliqué can be traced back to ancient times, where it was used by different cultures around the world. In Egypt, appliqué was used to decorate clothing and household items. In China, it was used to create intricate designs on silk garments. In Europe, appliqué was commonly used in tapestries and wall hangings.

The process of appliqué involves cutting out fabric shapes and attaching them to a base fabric using various stitching techniques. The fabric shapes can be cut by hand or using templates, and they can be made from different types of fabric, such as cotton, silk, or felt. The shapes can be simple or complex, depending on the desired design.

There are several methods of attaching the fabric shapes to the base fabric. One common method is hand stitching, where the fabric shapes are sewn onto the base fabric using a needle and thread. This method allows for precise control and detail in the design. Another method is machine stitching, where the fabric shapes are sewn onto the base fabric using a sewing machine. This method is faster and more efficient, especially for larger projects.

Appliqué can be used to create a wide range of designs and patterns. It can be used to add decorative elements to clothing, such as flowers, animals, or geometric shapes. It can also be used to create intricate designs on quilts, pillows, or wall hangings. The possibilities are endless, and appliqué allows for endless creativity and personalization.

In addition to fabric, other materials can also be used in appliqué. For example, beads, sequins, or ribbons can be added to enhance the design and add texture. These additional materials can be sewn onto the fabric shapes or attached using adhesive.

Learning appliqué can be a fun and rewarding experience. It allows individuals to express their creativity and create unique and personalized designs. There are many resources available, such as books, online tutorials, and classes, that can help beginners learn the basics of appliqué and develop their skills.

In conclusion, appliqué is a versatile and creative technique that allows individuals to add unique designs and patterns to fabric.

Appliqué: A Colorful Tapestry of Fabric Art: Appliqué is a vibrant and intricate form of fabric art that involves the process of sewing or attaching small pieces of fabric onto a larger piece to create a design or pattern. This technique has been used for centuries in various cultures around the world to embellish clothing, accessories, and home decor items.

The word "appliqué" is derived from the French word "appliquer," which means "to apply." In this art form, fabric pieces are cut into various shapes and sizes and then sewn onto a base fabric using a needle and thread. The pieces can be sewn directly onto the fabric or attached using an adhesive, such as fusible web or fabric glue.

One of the most fascinating aspects of appliqué is the wide range of materials that can be used. From cotton and silk to wool and leather, almost any type of fabric can be incorporated into an appliqué design. This allows artists to experiment with different textures, colors, and patterns, resulting in unique and visually stunning creations.

Appliqué can be done by hand or with the help of a sewing machine, depending on the complexity of the design and the artist's preference. Hand appliqué requires precision and patience, as each fabric piece needs to be carefully positioned and stitched onto the base fabric. Machine appliqué, on the other hand, allows for faster and more consistent stitching, making it a popular choice for larger projects or those with intricate details.

The history of appliqué can be traced back to ancient civilizations, such as the Egyptians and the Greeks, who used this technique to decorate their garments and textiles. In Asia, countries like India and China have a rich tradition of appliqué, with each region having its own unique style and motifs. In Africa, appliqué is often used to create vibrant and colorful designs on clothing and ceremonial textiles.

In contemporary times, appliqué has gained popularity among artists and crafters worldwide. It is not only used to enhance clothing and accessories but also to create wall hangings, quilts, and even three-dimensional sculptures. Many artists have pushed the boundaries of traditional appliqué by incorporating modern techniques, such as digital printing and laser cutting, into their work.

oroidery, and batik. Reverse appliqué allows for intricate and ailed designs to be created, and it can be done by hand or with the) of a sewing machine.

ddition to these forms of appliqué, there are also various techniques can be used to enhance the overall design. These include needle-, appliqué, where the fabric pieces are turned under and stitched by d using a needle and thread, and machine appliqué, where the ic pieces are attached using a sewing machine. Both techniques r different levels of precision and control, allowing for different cts to be achieved.

oliqué can be done on a wide range of fabrics, including cotton, silk, ol, and even leather. The choice of fabric can greatly impact the final k and feel of the appliqué design. Additionally, different types of ches and threads can be used to further enhance the design and add ture.

erall, appliqué is a versatile and creative sewing technique that ws for endless possibilities in design and style.

ope and Application in Modern Sewing:

he modern era, sewing has evolved from a basic skill to a complex I diverse craft. The scope and application of sewing have expanded nificantly, encompassing a wide range of industries and creative suits. From fashion design to home decor, sewing plays a crucial e in creating functional and aesthetically pleasing products.

Appliqué is not only a form of artistic expression b
preserve cultural heritage and traditions. Many indigei
continue to practice this art form, passing down the
designs from one generation to the next. By embracir
the beauty of appliqué, we can appreciate the skill a
goes into creating

Various Forms and Techniques of Appliqué in S
popular sewing technique that involves attaching fak
base fabric to create decorative designs or patterns.
forms and techniques of appliqué that can be used to
effects and styles.

One of the most common forms of appliqué is raw-e
this technique, fabric pieces are cut into desired s
attached to the base fabric using a sewing machine
The edges of the fabric pieces are left raw, which giv
and textured look to the design. Raw-edge appliqué
quilting projects and can be combined with other tec
patchwork to create intricate and visually appealing de

Another form of appliqué is turned-edge appliqué. I
fabric pieces are cut into desired shapes and then tui
the edges before being attached to the base fabric. Thi
and finished look as the raw edges are conceale
appliqué is commonly used in garment making and
hand or with the help of fusible web or adhesive.

Reverse appliqué is a technique where fabric pieces ai
of each other and then stitched together. The top layer
to reveal the fabric underneath, creating a contrasti
technique is often used in traditional textile arts s

er
de
he

In
th
tu
ha
fa
of
ef

Aļ
wo
lo
sti
te

O
all

S

In
ar
si
pι
ro

Appliqué is not only a form of artistic expression but also a way to preserve cultural heritage and traditions. Many indigenous communities continue to practice this art form, passing down their techniques and designs from one generation to the next. By embracing and celebrating the beauty of appliqué, we can appreciate the skill and creativity that goes into creating

Various Forms and Techniques of Appliqué in Sew: Appliqué is a popular sewing technique that involves attaching fabric pieces onto a base fabric to create decorative designs or patterns. There are various forms and techniques of appliqué that can be used to achieve different effects and styles.

One of the most common forms of appliqué is raw-edge appliqué. In this technique, fabric pieces are cut into desired shapes and then attached to the base fabric using a sewing machine or hand stitching. The edges of the fabric pieces are left raw, which gives a more rustic and textured look to the design. Raw-edge appliqué is often used in quilting projects and can be combined with other techniques such as patchwork to create intricate and visually appealing designs.

Another form of appliqué is turned-edge appliqué. In this technique, fabric pieces are cut into desired shapes and then turned under along the edges before being attached to the base fabric. This creates a clean and finished look as the raw edges are concealed. Turned-edge appliqué is commonly used in garment making and can be done by hand or with the help of fusible web or adhesive.

Reverse appliqué is a technique where fabric pieces are layered on top of each other and then stitched together. The top layer is then cut away to reveal the fabric underneath, creating a contrasting design. This technique is often used in traditional textile arts such as quilting, embroidery, and batik. Reverse appliqué allows for intricate and detailed designs to be created, and it can be done by hand or with the help of a sewing machine.

In addition to these forms of appliqué, there are also various techniques that can be used to enhance the overall design. These include needle-turn appliqué, where the fabric pieces are turned under and stitched by hand using a needle and thread, and machine appliqué, where the fabric pieces are attached using a sewing machine. Both techniques offer different levels of precision and control, allowing for different effects to be achieved.

Appliqué can be done on a wide range of fabrics, including cotton, silk, wool, and even leather. The choice of fabric can greatly impact the final look and feel of the appliqué design. Additionally, different types of stitches and threads can be used to further enhance the design and add texture.

Overall, appliqué is a versatile and creative sewing technique that allows for endless possibilities in design and style.

Scope and Application in Modern Sewing:

In the modern era, sewing has evolved from a basic skill to a complex and diverse craft. The scope and application of sewing have expanded significantly, encompassing a wide range of industries and creative pursuits. From fashion design to home decor, sewing plays a crucial role in creating functional and aesthetically pleasing products.

One of the primary applications of sewing in the modern world is in the fashion industry. Sewing is the foundation of garment construction, allowing designers to bring their creative visions to life. From haute couture to ready-to-wear, sewing techniques are used to create intricate and tailored garments that fit the human body perfectly. Sewing also enables the incorporation of various fabrics, textures, and embellishments, adding depth and character to fashion designs.

Beyond fashion, sewing has found its place in the world of home decor. From curtains and upholstery to bedding and pillows, sewing is essential for creating custom-made pieces that enhance the aesthetics of living spaces. Sewing techniques such as hemming, pleating, and quilting are used to add decorative elements and ensure the durability of home decor items. Additionally, sewing allows for the personalization of home decor, as individuals can choose fabrics, patterns, and colors that reflect their unique style and preferences.

Sewing also plays a vital role in the production of accessories and crafts. Handbags, wallets, and backpacks are often sewn together using specialized techniques to ensure durability and functionality. Sewing is also used in the creation of accessories such as hats, scarves, and gloves, adding a touch of individuality to personal style. Furthermore, sewing is a fundamental skill in the world of crafts, enabling the creation of items such as stuffed animals, quilts, and decorative ornaments.

In addition to its applications in fashion, home decor, and crafts, sewing has also found its place in various industries. The automotive industry, for example, relies on sewing for the production of car interiors, including seats, headliners, and door panels. Sewing is also used in the manufacturing of sports equipment, such as bags, gloves, and protective gear. The medical field also utilizes sewing techniques for the production of surgical gowns, masks, and other medical textiles.

The scope of sewing has expanded with the advancements in technology. Computerized sewing machines and software have revolutionized the craft, allowing for more precise and intricate stitching. These machines can execute complex embroidery designs, create intricate patterns, and even sew garments automatically.

Essential Tools and Materials for Appliqué in Sew: When it comes to appliqué in sewing, having the right tools and materials is essential to achieve the best results. Appliqué is a technique where fabric pieces are sewn onto a base fabric to create decorative designs or patterns. Whether you are a beginner or an experienced sewer, having the following tools and materials will make your appliqué projects easier and more enjoyable.

1. Fabric: The first and most important material for appliqué is the fabric itself. Choose a high-quality fabric that is suitable for your project. Cotton, linen, and silk are popular choices for appliqué as they are easy to work with and provide a smooth finish. Make sure to prewash and press your fabric before starting your project to prevent any shrinkage or distortion.

2. Fusible Web: Fusible web is a thin adhesive material that is used to attach the appliqué fabric to the base fabric. It comes in sheets or rolls and has a paper backing that can be easily peeled off. Fusible web allows you to create clean and precise appliqué shapes without the need for hand stitching. Look for a fusible web that is suitable for your fabric type and follow the manufacturer's instructions for application.

3. Appliqué Patterns: Having a variety of appliqué patterns is essential for creating different designs and shapes. You can find appliqué patterns in books, magazines, or online. Choose patterns that suit your style and skill level. Some patterns may require more intricate cutting and sewing techniques, so make sure to choose accordingly.

4. Appliqué Scissors: Appliqué scissors are small, sharp scissors with a curved blade. These scissors are designed to easily trim fabric close to the stitching line without cutting into the base fabric. They are a must-have tool for precise and clean appliqué work. Invest in a good pair of appliqué scissors that are comfortable to hold and have a sharp blade.

5. Appliqué Needles: Appliqué needles are thin and sharp needles that are specifically designed for appliqué work. They have a small eye and a sharp point, making it easier to stitch close to the edge of the appliqué fabric. Choose needles that are suitable for your fabric type and size. It's always a good idea to have a variety of needle sizes on hand to accommodate different fabric thicknesses.

6. Thread: Choosing the right thread for your appliqué project is crucial. Use a thread that matches the color of your appliqué fabric or opt for a contrasting color to create a decorative effect.

Choosing Fabrics and Threads for Appliqué in Sew: When it comes to appliqué in sewing, one of the most important aspects to consider is the choice of fabrics and threads. The right combination of these two elements can greatly enhance the overall look and durability of your appliqué project.

First and foremost, let's talk about fabrics. When selecting fabrics for appliqué, it is crucial to choose ones that are suitable for the purpose. Fabrics that are too thin or flimsy may not hold up well and can easily tear or fray. On the other hand, fabrics that are too thick or heavy may be difficult to work with and can create a bulky appearance.

Cotton fabrics are often a popular choice for appliqué due to their versatility and ease of use. They come in a wide range of colors and prints, making it easy to find the perfect fabric to complement your design. Additionally, cotton fabrics tend to be durable and hold up well to repeated washing and wear.

Another option to consider is using fusible webbing or interfacing. These materials can be ironed onto the back of your fabric, providing added stability and preventing fraying. This is especially useful when working with delicate or loosely woven fabrics.

In terms of thread selection, it is important to choose a thread that is strong and durable. Polyester or cotton threads are commonly used for appliqué projects, as they offer good strength and are less likely to break or fray. It is also recommended to use a thread that matches or complements the color of your fabric, as this will help create a seamless and professional-looking finish.

When it comes to the actual stitching, there are a few different techniques you can use. The most common method is to use a straight stitch or a zigzag stitch to secure the appliqué fabric to the base fabric. This can be done by hand or with a sewing machine, depending on your preference and the complexity of your design.

If you want to add more dimension and texture to your appliqué, you can also experiment with different types of stitches. For example, a satin stitch or a blanket stitch can create a decorative border around your appliqué, adding a touch of elegance and sophistication to your project.

In conclusion, choosing the right fabrics and threads for appliqué in sewing is crucial for achieving a successful and visually appealing result. By selecting fabrics that are suitable for the purpose and using strong and durable threads, you can ensure that your appliqué project will withstand the test of time.

Setting Up Your Sewing Space: Setting up your sewing space is an important step in creating a comfortable and efficient environment for your sewing projects. Whether you are a beginner or an experienced sewer, having a dedicated space for your sewing activities can greatly enhance your creativity and productivity. In this guide, we will provide you with detailed instructions on how to set up your sewing space to ensure that it meets all your needs and preferences.

Firstly, you need to choose the right location for your sewing space. Ideally, it should be a well-lit area with good ventilation. Natural light is preferable, as it allows you to see the true colors of your fabrics and threads. If natural light is not available, make sure to invest in good quality lighting fixtures that provide bright and even illumination. Additionally, ensure that the space is well-ventilated to prevent the accumulation of dust and fumes from your sewing activities.

Next, consider the size of your sewing space. It should be large enough to accommodate your sewing machine, cutting table, and storage units for your fabrics, threads, and other sewing supplies. If you have limited space, consider investing in space-saving furniture and storage solutions, such as foldable tables and wall-mounted shelves. This will help you maximize the available space and keep your sewing area organized and clutter-free.

When setting up your sewing machine, make sure to position it at a comfortable height and angle. The sewing machine should be placed on a sturdy table or sewing cabinet that provides a stable surface for your sewing activities. Adjust the height of the table or cabinet to ensure that your arms and wrists are in a relaxed and natural position while sewing. This will help prevent strain and fatigue during long sewing sessions.

In addition to your sewing machine, a cutting table is an essential component of your sewing space. It should be large enough to accommodate your fabric and provide ample space for cutting and measuring. Consider investing in a cutting mat that can be placed on top of the table to protect its surface and provide accurate measurements. You may also want to have a separate ironing station nearby for pressing seams and preparing your fabric before sewing.

Storage is another crucial aspect of your sewing space. Invest in storage units, such as shelves, drawers, and bins, to keep your fabrics, threads, patterns, and other sewing supplies organized and easily accessible. Categorize your supplies and label the storage containers to make it easier to find what you need.

Basic Techniques and Tips in Appliqué of Sew: Appliqué is a popular sewing technique that involves attaching fabric pieces onto a base fabric to create decorative designs or patterns. It is a versatile and creative way to add texture, color, and dimension to your sewing projects. Whether you are a beginner or an experienced sewer, here are some basic techniques and tips to help you master the art of appliqué.

1. Choose the Right Fabric: When selecting fabric for your appliqué project, it is important to choose fabrics that are compatible with each other. Opt for fabrics that have similar weights and textures to ensure a cohesive look. Additionally, consider the color and pattern of the fabric to ensure it complements your base fabric.

2. Prepare Your Fabric: Before you start appliquéing, it is crucial to prepare your fabric properly. This includes washing and ironing your fabric to remove any wrinkles or creases. If you are working with fusible web, make sure to follow the manufacturer's instructions for fusing it onto your fabric.

3. Trace and Cut Your Appliqué Shapes: To create your appliqué shapes, you can either use pre-made templates or draw your own. Trace the desired shape onto the wrong side of your fabric and cut it out carefully. It is important to cut accurately to ensure clean and precise edges.

4. Positioning and Pinning: Once you have your appliqué shapes ready, position them onto your base fabric to determine the desired placement. Use pins to secure the shapes in place temporarily. This will allow you to make any adjustments before permanently attaching them.

5. Appliqué Techniques: There are several techniques you can use to attach your appliqué shapes to the base fabric. One common method is using fusible web, which is an adhesive that bonds the fabric pieces together when heat is applied. Another technique is hand appliqué,

where you sew the shapes onto the fabric using a needle and thread. You can also use a sewing machine with a zigzag or satin stitch to secure the edges of the appliqué shapes.

6. Finishing Touches: Once your appliqué shapes are securely attached, you can add additional embellishments to enhance the design. This can include embroidery, beads, sequins, or decorative stitching. Be creative and experiment with different techniques to personalize your project.

7. Care and Maintenance: To ensure the longevity of your appliqué project, it is important to follow proper care and maintenance instructions. Always check the fabric care labels and wash your project accordingly.

Preparing Fabrics and Creating Appliqué Shapes in Sew:

A Comprehensive Guide

Introduction:

Sewing is a versatile craft that allows individuals to create unique and personalized items. One popular technique in sewing is appliqué, which involves attaching fabric shapes onto a base fabric to create decorative designs. In this guide, we will delve into the process of preparing fabrics and creating appliqué shapes, providing you with a step-by-step approach to achieve stunning results.

Section 1: Preparing Fabrics

1.1 Choosing the Right Fabrics:

Before starting any sewing project, it is crucial to select the appropriate fabrics for your appliqué. Consider the design, purpose, and desired outcome of your project. Fabrics with contrasting colors and textures often work well for appliqué, as they create visual interest. Ensure that the fabrics you choose are suitable for the intended use of the finished item, whether it be a quilt, clothing, or home decor.

1.2 Pre-Washing and Pressing:

To prevent any shrinkage or color bleeding, it is advisable to pre-wash your fabrics before beginning the appliqué process. Follow the manufacturer's instructions for washing and drying. Once the fabrics are clean and dry, press them with an iron to remove any wrinkles or creases. This step ensures that your appliqué shapes will adhere smoothly to the base fabric.

Section 2: Creating Appliqué Shapes

2.1 Choosing a Design:

Before cutting out your appliqué shapes, it is essential to have a clear design in mind. You can either draw your design freehand or use templates or stencils for more precise shapes. Consider the size, placement, and overall composition of your design. Experiment with different arrangements to find the most visually appealing option.

2.2 Transferring the Design:

Once you have finalized your design, transfer it onto the fabric that will be used for the appliqué shapes. There are several methods for transferring designs, including using tailor's chalk, fabric markers, or tracing paper. Choose the method that works best for your fabric and design. Ensure that the transferred lines are clear and visible.

2.3 Cutting Out the Appliqué Shapes:

Using sharp fabric scissors, carefully cut out the appliqué shapes along the transferred lines. Take your time and make precise cuts to achieve clean edges. If your design requires multiple layers or intricate details, consider using small embroidery scissors or a rotary cutter for more accuracy.

Techniques for Applying Appliqué Pieces to Base Fabric for Appliqué in Sew:

Appliqué is a popular technique in sewing that involves attaching smaller pieces of fabric onto a larger base fabric to create decorative designs or patterns. It adds texture, dimension, and visual interest to various sewing projects such as quilts, garments, and home decor items. To achieve a professional and polished look, it is essential to apply the appliqué pieces accurately and securely to the base fabric. In this article, we will explore different techniques for applying appliqué pieces to base fabric for appliqué in sewing.

1. Fusible Appliqué: This technique involves using fusible web or adhesive to attach the appliqué pieces to the base fabric. Fusible web is a thin, double-sided adhesive that is activated by heat. To apply fusible appliqué, start by tracing the appliqué design onto the paper side of the fusible web. Then, iron the fusible web onto the wrong side of the appliqué fabric. Once cooled, cut out the appliqué shape along the traced lines. Peel off the paper backing and position the appliqué piece onto the base fabric. Finally, press with an iron to fuse the appliqué piece onto the base fabric.

2. Needle-Turn Appliqué: This technique involves hand-sewing the appliqué pieces onto the base fabric using a needle and thread. To

begin, trace the appliqué design onto the wrong side of the appliqué fabric. Cut out the shape, leaving a small seam allowance. Next, fold the seam allowance under the shape and press it with an iron. Pin the folded edge in place and use a small, sharp needle to hand-sew the appliqué piece onto the base fabric. This technique requires precision and patience but results in a clean and seamless finish.

3. Raw-Edge Appliqué: This technique involves attaching the appliqué pieces to the base fabric with a raw, unfinished edge. It creates a more casual and textured look. To start, trace the appliqué design onto the wrong side of the appliqué fabric. Cut out the shape, leaving a small seam allowance. Position the appliqué piece onto the base fabric and secure it with pins or temporary fabric adhesive. Use a sewing machine or hand-stitching to sew around the edges of the appliqué piece, leaving the raw edge exposed. This technique works well with fabrics that do not fray easily.

Stitching Techniques in Appliqué: Stitching techniques in appliqué refer to the various methods and styles used to attach fabric pieces onto a base fabric in order to create a decorative design or pattern. Appliqué is a popular technique in sewing and quilting, where fabric shapes are cut out and then stitched onto a larger fabric piece to create a layered and textured effect.

There are several different stitching techniques that can be used in appliqué, each with its own unique characteristics and effects. One of the most common techniques is the blanket stitch, which is a simple and versatile stitch that can be used to secure the edges of the appliqué fabric to the base fabric. The blanket stitch creates a neat and decorative finish, with the stitches forming a series of loops along the edge of the fabric.

Another popular stitching technique in appliqué is the satin stitch. This stitch is used to completely cover the raw edges of the appliqué fabric, creating a smooth and seamless appearance. The satin stitch is often used for more intricate designs or when a more polished and refined look is desired. It requires precision and patience, as the stitches need to be close together and evenly spaced to achieve a professional finish.

In addition to the blanket stitch and satin stitch, there are other stitching techniques that can be used in appliqué, such as the running stitch, whip stitch, and ladder stitch. The running stitch is a basic and versatile stitch that can be used to attach the appliqué fabric to the base fabric, while the whip stitch is a quick and easy stitch that is often used for joining fabric pieces together. The ladder stitch, on the other hand, is a nearly invisible stitch that is used to close the opening left for turning or stuffing an appliqué piece.

When choosing a stitching technique for appliqué, it is important to consider the desired effect and the type of fabric being used. Some fabrics may require a specific stitching technique to ensure that the appliqué piece is securely attached and does not fray or unravel over time. Additionally, the choice of thread color can also have an impact on the overall appearance of the appliqué design, as it can either blend in or contrast with the fabric colors.

Overall, stitching techniques in appliqué play a crucial role in creating visually appealing and durable designs. Whether using the blanket stitch, satin stitch, or other stitching techniques, the key is to carefully select the appropriate technique for the desired effect and fabric type, and to execute the stitches with precision and attention to detail.

Exploring Different Styles of Appliqué: Appliqué is a decorative technique that involves attaching fabric pieces onto a base fabric to create a design or pattern. It is a versatile and creative way to add texture, color, and dimension to various projects such as quilts, clothing, home decor items, and accessories. There are different styles of appliqué that can be explored to achieve different effects and aesthetics.

One style of appliqué is raw-edge appliqué, also known as fused appliqué. This technique involves cutting out fabric shapes and attaching them to the base fabric using an adhesive, such as fusible web or glue. The edges of the fabric pieces are left raw, which adds a rustic and textured look to the design. Raw-edge appliqué is popular for creating contemporary and whimsical designs, as it allows for more freedom in shape and placement of the fabric pieces.

Another style of appliqué is turned-edge appliqué, which involves folding the fabric edges under and hand or machine stitching them onto the base fabric. This technique creates a clean and polished look, as the folded edges are neatly secured. Turned-edge appliqué is often used for creating intricate and detailed designs, as it allows for precise placement and control over the fabric pieces. It is a traditional and timeless style of appliqué that can be seen in heirloom quilts and vintage-inspired projects.

Reverse appliqué is a unique style of appliqué that involves layering fabric pieces and cutting away the top layers to reveal the fabric underneath. This technique creates a negative space effect, where the base fabric becomes the focal point of the design. Reverse appliqué is often used for creating bold and graphic designs, as it allows for contrasting colors and textures to be showcased. It can be done by hand or machine, and is a great way to add visual interest and depth to appliqué projects.

In addition to these styles, there are also various techniques and variations that can be explored within each style of appliqué. For example, needle-turn appliqué is a hand stitching technique that involves using a needle to turn the fabric edges under as you stitch them onto the base fabric. This technique requires precision and patience, but it allows for a seamless and invisible finish. Machine appliqué, on the other hand, involves using a sewing machine to stitch the fabric pieces onto the base fabric. This technique is faster and more efficient, making it a popular choice for larger projects or when time is limited.

Working with Layering and Textures for Appliqué in Sew: Working with layering and textures for appliqué in sewing involves a creative and intricate process that adds depth and visual interest to your fabric projects. Appliqué is a technique where fabric pieces are attached to a base fabric to create a design or pattern. By incorporating layering and textures, you can elevate your appliqué work to a whole new level.

Layering is a fundamental aspect of appliqué that allows you to build dimension and complexity in your designs. It involves placing multiple fabric pieces on top of each other, creating a layered effect. This technique can be used to add depth to your appliqué by creating shadows and highlights. For example, if you are creating a flower design, you can layer different shades of fabric petals to give the illusion of depth and dimension.

Textures play a crucial role in adding visual interest and tactile appeal to your appliqué work. By using fabrics with different textures, such as velvet, satin, or lace, you can create a contrast between the base fabric and the appliqué pieces. This contrast adds a dynamic element to your design, making it visually captivating. Additionally, textures can also be created through various stitching techniques, such as embroidery or quilting, which add a three-dimensional quality to your appliqué.

To work with layering and textures for appliqué, you will need to consider a few key factors. Firstly, choose fabrics that complement each other and create a harmonious color palette. This will ensure that the layers and textures blend seamlessly together. Additionally, consider the scale and size of your appliqué pieces. Different sizes and shapes can be layered to create interesting patterns and designs.

When it comes to attaching the appliqué pieces to the base fabric, there are several techniques you can use. One common method is fusible appliqué, where a heat-activated adhesive is applied to the back of the fabric pieces and then ironed onto the base fabric. This technique is quick and easy, but it may not be suitable for all fabrics or designs. Another option is hand stitching, which allows for more control and precision. This method is ideal for intricate designs or delicate fabrics.

Once your appliqué pieces are attached, you can further enhance the layering and textures through embellishments. This can include adding beads, sequins, or even additional fabric pieces to create more depth and visual interest. Experiment with different techniques and materials to find what works best for your design.

Enhancing Appliqué with Embellishments: Enhancing Appliqué with Embellishments is a creative and artistic technique that adds an extra layer of beauty and intricacy to appliqué designs. Appliqué itself is the process of sewing fabric pieces onto a larger fabric background to create a decorative design or pattern. However, by incorporating embellishments into the appliqué process, the final result becomes even more visually stunning and unique.

Embellishments can include a wide range of materials and techniques, such as beads, sequins, embroidery threads, ribbons, lace, and even small trinkets or charms. These elements are carefully selected and strategically placed onto the appliqué design to enhance its overall aesthetic appeal. The addition of embellishments not only adds texture and dimension to the design but also allows for personalization and customization, making each appliqué piece truly one-of-a-kind.

One of the key benefits of enhancing appliqué with embellishments is the ability to create a focal point or highlight certain areas of the design. For example, by adding beads or sequins to specific parts of the appliqué, such as flower petals or leaves, these elements can catch the light and draw attention to those areas. This technique adds depth and visual interest to the overall composition, making it more visually captivating.

Furthermore, embellishments can also be used to create intricate patterns or motifs within the appliqué design. For instance, by using embroidery threads or ribbons, one can create delicate and intricate stitches or patterns that complement the appliqué design. This level of detail and craftsmanship elevates the overall quality of the piece and showcases the artist's skill and creativity.

In addition to enhancing the visual appeal, embellishments can also serve a functional purpose. For example, by incorporating beads or sequins onto the edges of an appliqué design, it can help to reinforce and secure the fabric pieces in place. This added durability ensures that the appliqué piece will withstand regular wear and tear, making it suitable for various applications such as clothing, accessories, or home decor.

The process of enhancing appliqué with embellishments requires careful planning and execution. It involves selecting the right materials, colors, and textures that complement the appliqué design. Additionally, the placement and arrangement of the embellishments must be thoughtfully considered to achieve a balanced and harmonious composition. This attention to detail and precision is what sets apart a well-executed embellished appliqué piece from a mediocre one.

Appliqué Patterns

Introduction

Appliqué is a great way to add color and pizzazz to clothing, accessories and home décor items. It's easy to do, and with today's tools and materials, everyone can appliqué and turn out fresh and colorful projects in an afternoon.

Whether you sew or not, appliqué is fast, easy and adds a personal touch to your home and wardrobe. It's great for gifts and is simple enough that the kids can help, or even make their own creations.

The tools and materials are inexpensive, and there's a variety of ways to complete your projects. So, get out your scrap bag, scissors and iron, and start creating crafty keepsakes for yourself, your family and friends.

What Is Fusible Web?

Fusible web is a great product that can be used for hemming, repairs, crafting and, of course, appliqué. Created from a synthetic polymer that melts at a low temperature, it's a very thin layer of spun fibers that is available in rolls, sheets and tapes. When placed between two pieces of fabric, it bonds the layers together permanently with the application of heat.

It's available in a variety of weights produced by several manufacturers. You should use the weight that is similar to the fabric you are fusing. A heavier weight does not ensure a more permanent bond and can lead to problems if used incorrectly.

The kind of fusible web you'll use for appliqué projects come with a paper backing. Your pattern can be drawn directly on the paper, and the paper allows you to apply the web to the appliqué piece before fusing the two fabric layers together.

How To Appliqué With Fusible Transfer Web

With today's fusible transfer web, appliqué is a simple craft that anyone can easily learn. There's a number of brands and weights of fusible web available, so you should have no problem finding it at your local craft shop or fabric store.

As it becomes hard after it has been melted, heavy transfer web is not always a guarantee of a stronger bond. You should use the weight that is recommended by the manufacturer for the type of fabric you're using. To ensure your fabric fuses properly to the web, wash your cloth before using to remove any sizing.

First, choose your design. Besides the designs in this book, the internet is a wonderful place for royalty-free clip art you can download and print out. Another good source of designs is children's coloring books. These shapes are usually simple and perfect to use for appliqué.

Trace your shape on the paper side of the fusible transfer web, and place it on the wrong side of the fabric you'll be using to appliqué. Make sure the fabric is slightly larger than the fusible web so you don't inadvertently fuse the web to your ironing board.

Follow the manufacturer's instructions for temperature recommendations and ironing time.

Now that you've fused the web to the fabric, cut along the lines you've traced on the paper. Peel off the paper and position the appliqué on your garment. Follow the manufacturer's temperature recommendation and iron in place.

If the item is for a wall decoration and won't be laundered, that's all there is to it. If the appliqué is on an item of clothing or something that will get a lot of wear, you should stitch the edges. If you just want to prevent the edges from fraying, you can paint the cut edge with fabric paint or clear acrylic medium.

Hand Appliqué vs. Machine Appliqué

Now that you've gotten your appliqué adhered to your piece, you can either consider it complete, sew the border by hand or sew the edges with your sewing machine. Part of your decision is the end use of the item; personal preference and the degree of complexity are other factors.

If you want a handcrafted, homey look to your piece, hand stitching the edges of your appliqué is a good option. You can use a variety of threads and yarns like wool or acrylic crewel yarn, embroidery floss or metallic threads. Unusual fibers like raffia or twine give an interesting and unique look.

You can use a simple blanket stitch, or you can get fancy with embroidery stitches such as a chain stitch, cross stitch, fly stitch or lazy daisy stitch. Use different stitches for different areas of the appliqué pieces and contrasting colors to add texture and pizzazz.

If you use your sewing machine to edge your appliqué, you'll probably use a zigzag or satin stitch. A zigzag stitch will take less time, but it won't conceal the edges. A satin stitch will conceal the appliqué edges and make the item far more durable. You can vary the width of the satin stitch or zigzag stitch, and a variety of widths and thread colors will add interest to the piece.

What Can I Appliqué?

If it's cloth, cute and could use a little extra zing, it's a potential for the appliqué fairy! You can appliqué almost anything. It just depends on what fabrics you select for your appliqué and the method you use to attach your pieces.

If you're planning to appliqué new clothing, wash the garment. This will pre-shrink the item and remove any sizing that may interfere with the fusible web bonding process. Your appliqué material should be pre-washed as well.

If the item is not washable, such as a home décor item, be especially careful that the fusible web bonds securely. Delicate items require extra care, as the heat of the iron may damage them. For this type of item, use the minimum heat setting required to fuse the fabric, and use a pressing cloth to protect the fibers.

You can add appliqué to pillows, purses and tote bags, jackets, scarves and table linens. Customize guest towels, kitchen accessories or even curtains and pet products. Once you start, you'll find appliqué opportunities everywhere!

Homespun Holidays

Everyone loves to decorate for Christmas. Decorate yourself as well as your home with fun and fanciful appliqués for shirts, sweatshirts, pillows, towels and children's items.

Angels, snowmen and poinsettias add a special holiday look that everyone will enjoy. Use specialty Christmas fabrics, or use up some of the scraps in your stash to create festive outfits and accessories to dress up yourself and your home for the holidays.

HOMESPUN HOLIDAYS

Angel Pattern

If we were all a little more like Angels, earth would be a little more like heaven. You will be a hit in this angelic design - sew it on a denim shirt or jumper. Angel pattern can also be used on a jacket or pillow.

Print the full size angel patterns:
www.FreeApplique.com/Patterns/angelpat1.html
www.FreeApplique.com/Patterns/angelpat2.html

Supplies:

Denim shirt
Small amounts of fabric
Thread to match the fabric
Two small buttons

Fusible web

Angel Shirt Instructions

Follow the fusible web manufacturer's iron on instructions and iron the fusible web on the wrong side of the fabric.

From the fabric with the fusible web applied, cut a piece 17 1/2" by 1 1/4" wide. This will be the collar piece.

Trace the pattern pieces on the fusible web paper backing and cut out all pieces. Peel the fusible web paper backing from all pieces. Position each piece on shirt with right side of the fabric up. Iron pattern pieces on the shirt as directed for the fusible web.

Sew pieces on with a medium tight zigzag stitch. You need to sew a small tight zigzag stitch from each of the three small stars to her hand.

When you are done, sew the two small buttons on the angel's dress. Use a black fabric marker pen to make eyes on the angel's face.

Snowman Applique Shirt

Here is a quick and easy project that will add a touch of winter to any denim shirt. The applique would also look nice on a Christmas stocking.

Print the full size applique patterns:
FreeApplique.com/applique.data/snowman1.jpg

Supplies:

Denim shirt
Fabric scraps
Thread to match
Fusible web

Snowman Applique Shirt Instructions

Follow the fusible web manufacturer's iron on instructions and iron the fusible web on the wrong side of the fabric.

From the fabric with the fusible web applied, cut two pieces 17 1/2" long by 1 1/4" wide. One will be for the collar and the other one will be used on a long sleeve shirt on the cuffs.

Trace the pattern pieces on the fusible web paper backing and cut out all pieces. Peel the fusible web paper backing from all pieces. Position each piece on shirt with right side of the fabric up. Iron pattern pieces on the shirt as directed for the fusible web.

Sew pieces on with a medium tight zigzag stitch.

Collar Width

Christmas Applique Shirt

Behind every seamstress is a huge pile of fabric.

Print the full size applique patterns:
FreeApplique.com/applique.data/2snowmen1.jpg
FreeApplique.com/applique.data/2snowmen2.jpg

Supplies:

Denim shirt
Fabric scraps
Thread to match
Fusible web

Christmas Applique Shirt Instructions

Follow the fusible web manufacturer's iron on instructions and iron the fusible web on the wrong side of the fabric.

From the fabric with the fusible web applied, cut two pieces 17 1/2" long by 1 1/4" wide. One will be for the collar and the other one will be used on a long sleeve shirt on the cuffs.

Trace the pattern pieces on the fusible web paper backing and cut out all pieces. Peel the fusible web paper backing from all pieces. Position each piece on shirt with right side of the fabric up. Iron pattern pieces on the shirt as directed for the fusible web.

Sew pieces on with a medium tight zigzag stitch.

Poinsettia Sweatshirt Pattern

Friends are like fabric,
You can never have enough!

Print the full size applique patterns:
www.FreeApplique.com/applique.data/poinsettapattern.gif

Supplies:

Sweatshirt
Fabric scraps
Thread to match fabric
Fusible web

Poinsettia Christmas Sweatshirt Instructions

Follow the fusible web manufacturer's iron on instructions and iron the fusible web on the wrong side of the fabric.

Trace the pattern pieces on the fusible web paper backing and cut out all pieces. Peel the fusible web paper backing from all pieces. Position each piece on sweatshirt. Iron pattern pieces on the sweatshirt as directed for the fusible web.

Sew the pattern pieces on with a medium zigzag stitch.

BIRDS AND BIRDHOUSES

Birdhouse patterns are charming and whimsical additions that add color and texture. You can use just about any fabric to create your multi-colored birdhouse, and they're a great way to use up scraps.

Don't limit your palette to just a couple of fabrics. Use solids, prints, florals and stripes to create fanciful birdhouses that brighten up a plain shirt or add color and pattern to home decorating items.

Birdhouse Trio Sweatshirt Pattern

My husband lets me buy all the fabric I can hide.

Print the full size applique patterns:
FreeApplique.com/applique.data/fencess1.jpg
FreeApplique.com/applique.data/fencess2.jpg

Supplies:

Sweatshirt
Fabric scraps

Thread to match fabric
Fusible web

Birdhouse Trio Sweatshirt Instructions

Follow the fusible web manufacturer's iron on instructions and iron the fusible web on the wrong side of the fabric.

Trace the pattern pieces on the fusible web paper backing and cut out all pieces. Peel the fusible web paper backing from all pieces. Position each piece on sweatshirt. Iron pattern pieces on the sweatshirt as directed for the fusible web. Sew the pattern pieces on with a medium zigzag stitch.

Bird Sweatshirt Jacket

I got a sewing machine for my husband. Good trade, eh?

This birdhouse scene would be stunning on a sweatshirt jacket, denim shirt or wall quilt.

Print the full size applique patterns:
FreeApplique.com/Patterns/birdjacketpat1.html
FreeApplique.com/Patterns/birdjacketpat2.html

Supplies:

Sweatshirt jacket
Fabric scraps
5 buttons
Thread to match fabric
Fusible web

Bird Sweatshirt Jacket Instructions

This design is on a sweatshirt jacket but can be put on a plain sweatshirt or a denim shirt as well.

Follow the fusible web manufacturer's iron on instructions and iron the fusible web on the wrong side of the fabric.

Trace the pattern pieces on the fusible web paper backing with a pencil and cut out all pieces. Position each piece on sweatshirt jacket with right side of the fabric up.

Iron pattern pieces on the sweatshirt as directed for the fusible web.

Sew the pattern pieces on with a medium zigzag stitch. Now sew some buttons on the birdhouses.

Sew the pattern pieces on with a medium zigzag stitch. Now sew some buttons on the birdhouses.

Lacy Birdhouse Pattern

When life hands you scraps, applique a shirt!

Print the full size applique patterns:
FreeApplique.com/applique.data/laceyss1.jpg
FreeApplique.com/applique.data/laceyss2.jpg

Supplies:

Sweatshirt
Fabric scraps
Thread to match fabric
Fusible web
Scraps of Lace

Lacy Birdhouse Sweatshirt Instructions

Follow the fusible web manufacturer's iron on instructions and iron the fusible web on the wrong side of the fabric.

Trace the pattern pieces on the fusible web paper backing and cut out all pieces. Peel the fusible web paper backing from all pieces. Position each piece on sweatshirt. Iron pattern pieces on the sweatshirt as directed for the fusible web. Sew the pattern pieces on with a medium zigzag stitch.

After sewing everything onto the sweatshirt, measure scraps of lace to put on the roof and sew them to the sweatshirt. The lace should be wide enough to cover just the roof of the birdhouses.

Hummingbird Shirt

I'd rather be stitchin' than in the kitchen.

Print the full size applique patterns:

FreeApplique.com/Patterns/hummingbirdpat.html

Supplies:

Denim shirt
Fabric scraps
Thread to match
Fusible web

Hummingbird Shirt Instructions

Follow the fusible web manufacturer's iron on instructions and iron the fusible web on the wrong side of the fabric.

From the fabric with the fusible web applied, cut two pieces 17 1/2" long by 1 1/4" wide. One will be for the collar and the other one will be used on a long sleeve shirt on the cuffs.

Trace the pattern pieces on the fusible web paper backing and cut out all pieces. Peel the fusible web paper backing from all pieces. Position each piece on shirt with right side of the fabric up. Iron pattern pieces on the shirt as directed for the fusible web.

Sew pieces on with a medium tight zigzag stitch.

Collar

Cats and Birdhouses Shirt

Sew much fabric....sew little time.

Print the full size applique patterns:

www.FreeApplique.com/Patterns/catbirdpat1.html
www.FreeApplique.com/Patterns/catbirdpat2.html
www.FreeApplique.com/Patterns/catbirdpat3.html

Supplies:

Denim shirt
Fabric scraps
Thread to match
Fusible web

Cats and Birdhouses Shirt Instructions

Follow the fusible web manufacturer's iron on instructions and iron the fusible web on the wrong side of the fabric.

From the fabric with the fusible web applied, cut one piece 17 1/2" long by 1 1/4" wide. This piece will be used on the collar.

Trace the pattern pieces on the fusible web paper backing and cut out all pieces. Peel the fusible web paper backing from all pieces. Position each piece on shirt with right side of the fabric up. Iron pattern pieces on the shirt as directed for the fusible web.

Sew pieces on with a medium tight zigzag stitch.

Sew pieces on with a medium tight zigzag stitch.

Birdhouse Sweatshirt Pattern

Add a homespun touch to any sweatshirt. The birdhouse pattern would also be great to use for applique on quilts.

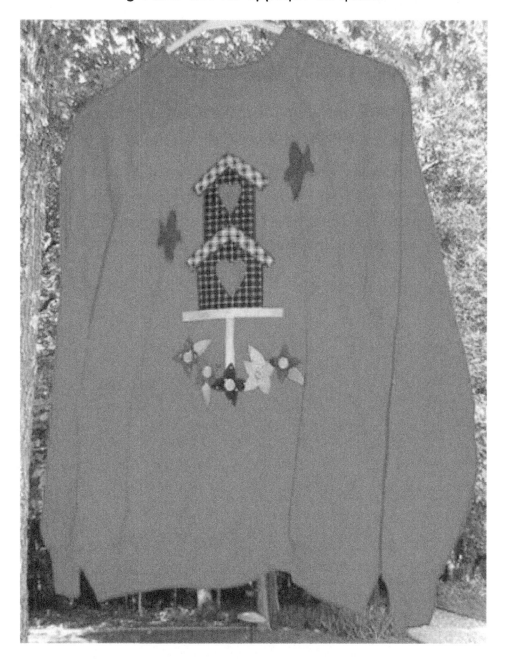

Print the full size applique patterns:
FreeApplique.com/applique.data/redss1aa.jpg
FreeApplique.com/applique.data/redss2aa.jpg

Supplies:

Sweatshirt
Fabric scraps
Thread to match fabric
Fusible web

Birdhouse Sweatshirt Instructions

Follow the fusible web manufacturer's iron on instructions and iron the fusible web on the wrong side of the fabric.

Trace the pattern pieces on the fusible web paper backing and cut out all pieces. Peel the fusible web paper backing from all pieces. Position each piece on sweatshirt. Iron pattern pieces on the sweatshirt as directed for the fusible web.

Sew the pattern pieces on with a medium zigzag stitch.

YoYo Bird Applique Pattern

Any day spent sewing is a good day.
Sew this free birdhouse applique quilt pattern on a shirt or wall quilt. Cute
birdhouse pattern uses yoyos for flowers.

Print the full size applique patterns:
www.FreeApplique.com/Patterns/birdpat1aa.html
www.FreeApplique.com/Patterns/birdpat2aa.html

Supplies:

Denim shirt
Fabric scraps
Thread to match fabric
4 large buttons
4 medium buttons
Fusible web

YoYo Birdhouse Instructions

Follow the fusible web manufacturer's iron on instructions and iron the fusible web on the wrong side of the fabric.

From the fabric with the fusible web applied, cut a piece 17 1/2" long and 1 1/4" wide. This will be the collar piece.

Trace the pattern pieces on the fusible web paper backing and cut out all pieces. Peel the fusible web paper backing from all pieces. Position each piece on shirt with the right side up. Iron patterns on as directed for the fusible web.

Sew pieces on with a medium width, tight zigzag stitch. Sew buttons on the birdhouse.

To make yoyo's, fold the edges 1/4" and run a gathering stitch along edge. Pull thread to make a yoyo and knot thread on bottom of yoyo. Sew yoyos on the shirt with a medium button in the center.

Sunflower Shirt

Friendships are sewn one stitch at a time.

Print the full size applique patterns:

FreeApplique.com/applique.data/sunflower1aa.gif
FreeApplique.com/applique.data/sunflower2aa.gif

Supplies:

Denim Shirt
Fabric scraps
Fusible web
Thread to match fabric

Sunflower Shirt Instructions

Follow the fusible web manufacturer's iron on instructions and iron the fusible web on the wrong side of the fabric.

From the fabric with the fusible web applied, cut a piece 17 1/2" long and 1 1/4" wide. This will be the collar piece.

Trace the pattern pieces on the fusible web paper backing and cut out all pieces. Peel the fusible web paper backing from all pieces. Position each piece on shirt with right side of the fabric up. Iron patterns on as directed for the fusible web.

Sew pieces on with a medium width tight zigzag stitch.

Butterfly Applique

BUTTERFLY APPLIQUE

Add all the colors of the rainbow with fanciful butterflies. Embellish a shirt, skirt or a pair of little girl's pants with fluttering butterflies. Butterflies are great for adding color and pattern and can be a creative starting point for a decorating theme in a little girl's bedroom or a guest bathroom.

Use delicate florals and bold solid fabrics to create a combination that's eye-catching and colorful. Small or large, these appliqués can be applied as an overall design or as a single embellishment on a small item like a hat or finger towel.

Butterfly Applique Shirt

Ready...Set...Sew!

Print the full size applique patterns:

FreeApplique.com/Patterns/butterflypat1.html

FreeApplique.com/Patterns/butterflypat2.html

Supplies:

Denim shirt
Fabric scraps
Thread to match fabric
Fusible web

Butterfly Shirt Instructions

Follow the fusible web manufacturer's iron on instructions and iron the fusible web on the wrong side of the fabric.

From the fabric with the fusible web applied, cut a piece 17 1/2" long by 1 1/4" wide. This will be the collar piece.

Trace the pattern pieces on the fusible web paper backing and cut out all pieces. Peel the fusible web paper backing from all pieces. Position each piece on shirt with right side of the fabric up. Iron patterns on as directed for the fusible web.

Sew pieces on with a medium width tight zigzag stitch.

When you are done sewing the pieces on, you are ready to start making the body and antennas on the butterflies and also the holes for the butterfly house.

For the butterfly house, you will need black thread and the largest width on your machine with a tight zigzag stitch.

For the bodies of the butterflies, use a large tight zigzag stitch and for the antennas use a very small tight zigzag stitch.

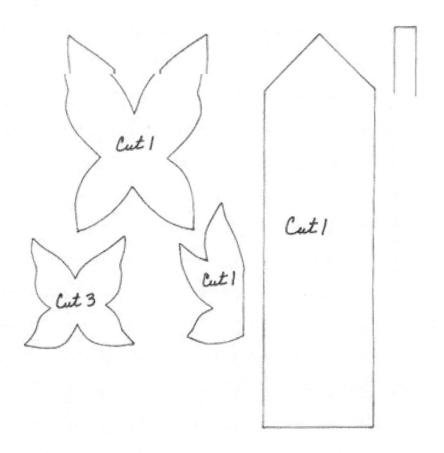

Cut 1

Cut 3

Cut 1

Cut 1

Butterfly House Shirt

Print the full size applique patterns:
FreeApplique.com/applique.data/butterss1.jpg

Supplies:

Denim shirt
Fabric scraps
Thread to match fabric
Fusible web

Butterfly House Shirt Instructions

Follow the fusible web manufacturer's iron on instructions and iron the fusible web on the wrong side of the fabric.

Trace the pattern pieces on the fusible web paper backing and cut out all the pieces. Peel the fusible web paper backing from all pieces. Position each piece on shirt with right side of the fabric up. Iron patterns on as directed for the fusible web.

Sew pieces on with a medium width tight zigzag stitch.

When you are done sewing the pieces on the sweatshirt, you are ready to start making the body and antennas on the butterflies.

For the butterfly house, you will need black thread and the largest width on your machine with a tight zigzag.

For the bodies of the butterfly, you will need a large tight zigzag and for the antenna's you will need a very small tight zigzag stitch.

HEART PATTERNS

You don't need to wait for Valentine's Day to start sewing hearts. Hearts are one of the most popular decorating themes for home and apparel, so you know you won't miss the mark when you appliqué hearts.

Funky, traditional, contemporary or eclectic, hearts of all shapes and sizes are great to add on gifts, clothing for everyone and accessories for the home. Let your imagination and scrap bin run wild with all the colors and patterns.

Lots o' Red Shirt

She who dies with the most fabric....wins.

Print the full size applique patterns:
FreeApplique.com/applique.data/redstar1a.gif
FreeApplique.com/applique.data/redstar2a.gif

Supplies:

Denim Shirt
Fabric scraps
Thread to match fabric
Fusible web

Lots O' Red Shirt Instructions

Follow the fusible web manufacturer's iron on instructions and iron the fusible web on the wrong side of the fabric.

From the fabric with the fusible web applied, cut a piece 17 1/2" long by 1 1/4" wide. This will be the collar piece.

Trace the pattern pieces on the fusible web paper backing and cut out all pieces. Peel the fusible web paper backing from all pieces. Position each piece on shirt with right side of the fabric up. Iron pattern pieces on the shirt as directed for the fusible web.

Sew pieces on with a tight zigzag stitch.

Cut 1

Maroon Applique Shirt

If I stitch fast enough does it count as an aerobic exercise?

Print the full size applique patterns:
FreeApplique.com/applique.data/maroon1.gif
FreeApplique.com/applique.data/maroon2.gif

Supplies:

Maroon shirt or a denim shirt
Fabric scraps
Thread to match fabric
Fusible web

Maroon Applique Shirt Instructions

Follow the fusible web manufacturer's iron on instructions and iron the fusible web on the wrong side of the fabric.

From the fabric with the fusible web applied, cut two pieces 17 1/2" long by 1 1/4" wide. One will be for the collar and the other one will be used on the cuffs of the long sleeve shirt.

Trace the pattern pieces on the fusible web paper backing and cut out all pieces. Peel the fusible web paper backing from all pieces. Position each piece on the shirt with the right side of the fabric up. Iron the pattern pieces on the shirt as directed for the fusible web.

Sew pieces on with a medium tight zigzag stitch.

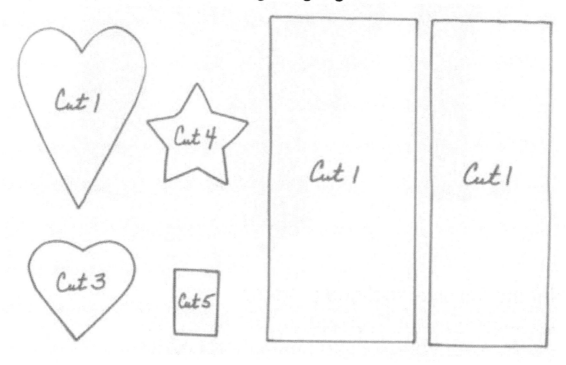

Hearts Denim Shirt

Itchin' to be Stitchin'.

Print the full size applique patterns:
FreeApplique.com/applique.data/grow1.gif
FreeApplique.com/applique.data/grow3.gif

FreeApplique.com/applique.data/grow2.gif

Supplies:

Denim Shirt
Fabric scraps
Thread to match fabric
Four medium buttons
21" of jute for bows
Fusible web

Growing Hearts Denim Shirt Instructions

Follow the fusible web manufacturer's iron on instructions and iron the fusible web on the wrong side of the fabric.

From the fabric with the fusible web applied, cut a piece 17 1/2" long and 1 1/4" wide. This will be the collar piece.

Trace the pattern pieces on the fusible web paper backing and cut out all pieces. Peel the fusible web paper backing from all pieces. Position each piece on shirt with right side of the fabric up. Iron patterns on as directed for the fusible web.

Sew pieces on with a medium width tight zigzag stitch.

Make three bows out of the jute. These go near the top of the three hearts on the right side of the shirt. Place a button on top of the jute bow and hand sew them both in place. Hand sew the other button on the large heart on the other side of the shirt.

This shirt looks nice with the Growing Hearts T-Shirt underneath.

This shirt looks nice with the Growing Hearts T-Shirt underneath.

Growing Hearts T-Shirt

When I learned how to sew...I forgot how to cook.

Print the full size applique patterns:

www.FreeApplique.com/applique.data/gh1.gif
www.FreeApplique.com/applique.data/gh4.gif
www.FreeApplique.com/applique.data/gh3.gif
www.FreeApplique.com/applique.data/gh2.gif

Supplies:

One T-Shirt
Fabric scraps
Thread to match fabric
Three medium buttons
21" of Jute for bows
Fusible web

Growing Hearts T-shirt Instructions

Follow the fusible web manufacturer's iron on instructions and iron the fusible web on the wrong side of the fabric.

Trace the pattern pieces on the fusible web paper backing and cut out all pieces. Remove fusible web from all pieces. Position each piece on T-shirt with right side of the pattern pieces up. Iron pattern pieces on as directed for the fusible web.

Sew pieces on with a medium width loose zigzag stitch.

Using jute, make three bows. These go on the hearts down the front of the T-shirt. Place a button on top of the jute bow and hand sew both in place.

Using jute, make three bows. These go on the hearts down the front of the T-shirt. Place a button on top of the jute bow and hand sew both in place.

Have a Heart Pattern

Print the full size applique patterns:
FreeApplique.com/applique.data/haveaheartpatt.jpg

Supplies:

Sweatshirt
Fabric scraps
Thread to match fabric
Fusible web
Purchased knit collar

Have a Heart Sweatshirt Instructions

Follow the fusible web manufacturer's iron on instructions and iron the fusible web on the wrong side of the fabric.

Trace the pattern pieces on the fusible web paper backing and cut out all pieces. Peel the fusible web paper backing from all pieces. Position each piece on the sweatshirt. Iron the pattern pieces on the sweatshirt as in the directions for the fusible web.

Sew the pattern pieces on with a medium zigzag stitch.

Hearts and Stars Sweatshirt Patterns

Will work for fabric!

Hearts and Stars Sweatshirts Pattern

Print the full size applique patterns:
www.FreeApplique.com/applique.data/starss.gif
www.FreeApplique.com/applique.data/heartss.gif

Supplies:

Sweatshirt
Fabric scraps
Thread to match fabric
Fusible web

Hearts and Stars Instructions

Follow the fusible web manufacturer's iron on instructions and iron the fusible web on the wrong side of the fabric.

Trace the pattern pieces on the fusible web paper backing and cut out all pieces. Peel the fusible web paper backing from all pieces.

Position each piece on sweatshirt. Iron pattern pieces on the sweatshirt as directed for the fusible web.

Sew the pattern pieces on with a medium zigzag stitch. I have put the same pattern on the back of the sweatshirt that is on the front.

Clover Shirt

One yard of fabric, like one cookie, is never enough.

Print the full size applique patterns:

FreeApplique.com/applique.data/clovershirtpattern2.jpg

Supplies:

Denim shirt
Fabric scraps
Thread to match
Fusible web

Clover Shirt Instructions

Follow the fusible web manufacturer's iron on instructions and iron the fusible web on the wrong side of the fabric.

From the fabric with the fusible web applied, cut two pieces 17 1/2" long by 1 1/4" wide. One will be for the collar and the other one will be used on a long sleeve shirt on the cuffs.

Trace the pattern pieces on the fusible web paper backing and cut out all pieces. Peel the fusible web paper backing from all pieces. Position each piece on shirt with right side of the fabric up. Iron pattern pieces on the shirt as directed for the fusible web.

Sew pieces on with a medium tight zigzag stitch.

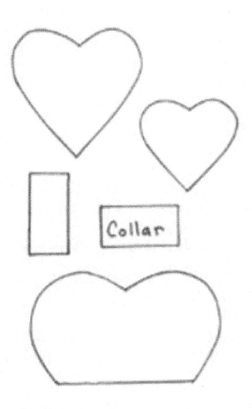

Collar

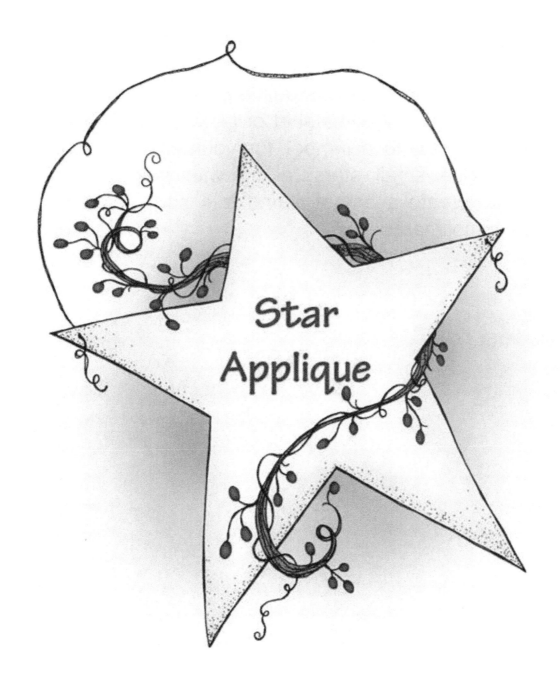

STAR APPLIQUE

You don't need to be patriotic to use stars. Star appliqués are a natural to add Independence Day fun to your summer home decorations, but don't stop there. Create colorful shirts and aprons, or decorate a set of picnic napkins with bright and spirited stars.

If you're a quilting fan, star quilting patterns make perfect appliqués to add to a sweatshirt or jacket. Add a Texas Star or patchwork star to a jumper for yourself or your favorite little one. Use small stars, along with hearts and other designs, to create a one-of-a-kind tote bag that will gather loads of compliments.

Lone Star Vest Pattern

Buttons and patches and the cold wind blowing
...the days pass quickly when I am sewing.

Print the full size applique patterns:
FreeApplique.com/applique.data/vest1.gif
FreeApplique.com/applique.data/vest2.gif

Supplies:

Vest
Fabric scraps

Thread to match fabric
Fusible web
Six small buttons

Lone Star Vest Instructions

Follow the fusible web manufacturer's iron on instructions and iron the fusible web on the wrong side of the fabric.

From the fabric with the fusible web applied, cut a piece 17 1/2" by 1 1/4" wide. This will be the collar piece.

Trace the pattern pieces on the fusible web paper backing and cut out all pieces. Remove fusible web from all pieces. Position each piece on vest with right side of the fabric up. Iron pattern pieces on as directed for the fusible web. Sew pieces on with a medium width tight zigzag stitch.

Sew buttons on all four corners of the large square. Sew a button on the other side of the shirt in each of the triangles.

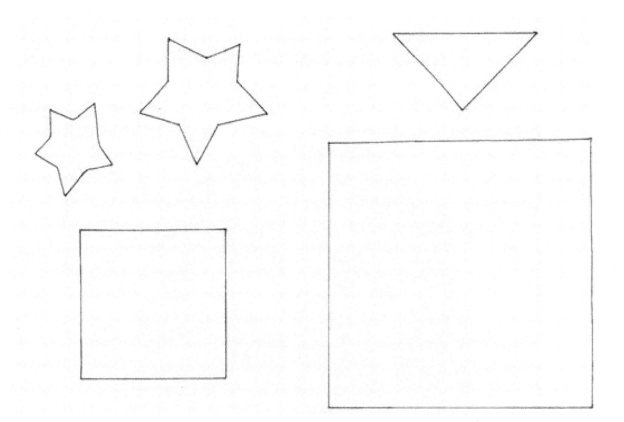

Star Light Star Bright Shirt

I'd rather be stitchin' than in the kitchen.

Print the full size applique patterns:
FreeApplique.com/applique.data/starlight1.gif
FreeApplique.com/applique.data/starlight2.gif
FreeApplique.com/applique.data/starlight3.gif

Supplies:

Denim shirt
Fabric scraps
Thread to match
Fusible web

Star Light Star Bright Shirt Instructions

Follow the fusible web manufacturer's iron on instructions and iron the fusible web on the wrong side of the fabric.

From the fabric with the fusible web applied, cut two pieces 17 1/2" long by 1 1/4" wide. One will be for the collar and the other one will be used on a long sleeve shirt on the cuffs.

Trace the pattern pieces on the fusible web paper backing and cut out all pieces. Peel the fusible web paper backing from all pieces. Position each piece on shirt with right side of the fabric up. Iron pattern pieces on the shirt as directed for the fusible web.

Sew pieces on with a medium tight zigzag stitch.

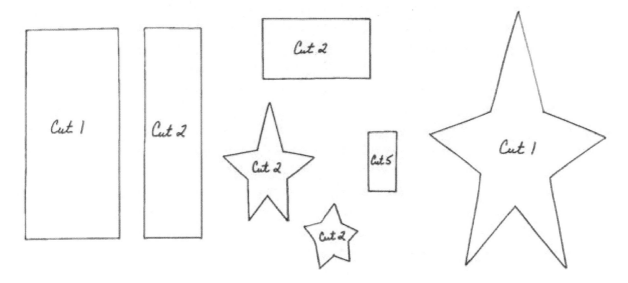

Star Log Shirt

A family stitched together with love, seldom unravels.

Print the full size applique patterns:
Freeapplique.com/applique.data/starshirt1.gif
Freeapplique.com/applique.data/starshirt2.gif

Supplies:

Denim shirt
Fabric scraps
Thread to match fabric
Six small buttons
Fusible web

Star Log Shirt Instructions

Follow the fusible web manufacturer's iron on instructions and iron the fusible web on the wrong side of the fabric.

From the fabric with the fusible web applied, cut a piece 17 1/2" long and 1 1/4" wide. This will be the collar piece.

Trace the pattern pieces on the fusible web paper backing and cut out all pieces. Peel the fusible web paper backing from all pieces. Position each piece on shirt with right side of the fabric up. Iron patterns on as directed for the fusible web.

Sew pieces on with a medium width tight zigzag stitch.

Sew a button on each of the large rectangles on top. Sew a button on two of the smaller rectangles on top.

Stars & Stripes T-Shirt

I was Cut out to be RICH, but I was Sewed up WRONG.

Stitch up this quick and easy T-shirt. This T-shirt looks great under the Star Log Denim shirt.

Print the full size applique patterns:
www.FreeApplique.com/applique.data/StarT1.gif
www.FreeApplique.com/applique.data/starT2.gif

Supplies:

T-Shirt
Fabric scraps
Thread to match fabric
Four small buttons
Fusible web

Stars & Stripes T-Shirt Instructions

Follow the fusible web manufacturer's iron on instructions and iron the fusible web on the wrong side of the fabric.

Trace the pattern pieces on the fusible web paper backing and cut out all pieces. Peel the fusible web paper backing from all pieces. Position each piece on shirt with right side of the fabric up. Iron patterns on as directed for the fusible web.

Sew pieces on with a medium width loose zigzag stitch.

Sew a button on the top of each large rectangles.

Sunburst Shirt

I'd rather be stitchin' than in the kitchen.

Print the full size applique patterns:
FreeApplique.com/Patterns/sunburstpat1.html
FreeApplique.com/Patterns/sunburstpat2.html

Supplies:

Denim shirt
Fabric scraps
Thread to match
Fusible web

Sunburst Shirt

Follow the fusible web manufacturer's iron on instructions and iron the fusible web on the wrong side of the fabric.

From the fabric with the fusible web applied, cut two pieces 17 1/2" long by 1 1/4" wide. One will be for the collar and the other one will be used on a long sleeve shirt on the cuffs.

Trace the pattern pieces on the fusible web paper backing and cut out all pieces. Peel the fusible web paper backing from all pieces. Position each piece on shirt with right side of the fabric up. Iron pattern pieces on the shirt as directed for the fusible web. Sew pieces on with a medium tight zigzag stitch.

Quilter's Star Pattern

Print the full size applique patterns:
FreeApplique.com/applique.data/quilterspattern.jpg

Supplies:

Sweatshirt
Fabric scraps
Thread to match fabric
Fusible web

Quilter's Star Sweatshirt Instructions

Follow the fusible web manufacturer's iron on instructions and iron the fusible web on the wrong side of the fabric.

Trace the pattern pieces on the fusible web paper backing and cut out all pieces. Peel the fusible web paper backing from all pieces. Position each piece on sweatshirt. Iron pattern pieces on the sweatshirt as directed for the fusible web.

Sew the pattern pieces on with a medium zigzag stitch.

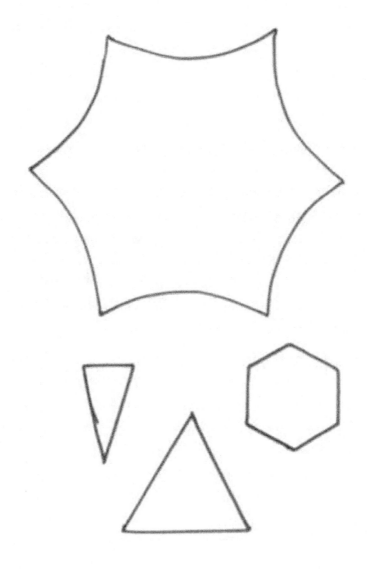

Country Stars Denim Shirt

Memories are stitched with love.
Sew this free applique pattern on a denim shirt, vest, or quilt.

Print the full size applique patterns:

FreeApplique.com/applique.data/countrystars1.jpg

Supplies:

Denim shirt
Fabric scraps
Thread to match fabric
Fusible web
Six small buttons

Country Stars Shirt Instructions

Follow the fusible web manufacturer's iron on instructions and iron the fusible web on the wrong side of the fabric.

From the fabric with the fusible web applied, cut a piece 17 1/2" long and 1 1/4" wide. This will be the collar piece.

Trace the pattern pieces on the fusible web paper backing and cut out all pieces. Remove fusible web from all pieces. Position each piece on shirt with right side of the fabric up. Iron pattern pieces on as directed for the fusible web. Sew pieces on with a medium width tight zigzag stitch. Or you can vary the stitch from tight to loose on different parts of the pattern pieces.

Sew buttons on all four corners of the large square. Sew a button on the other side of the shirt in each of the triangles.

You can mix and match different pieces of fabric.

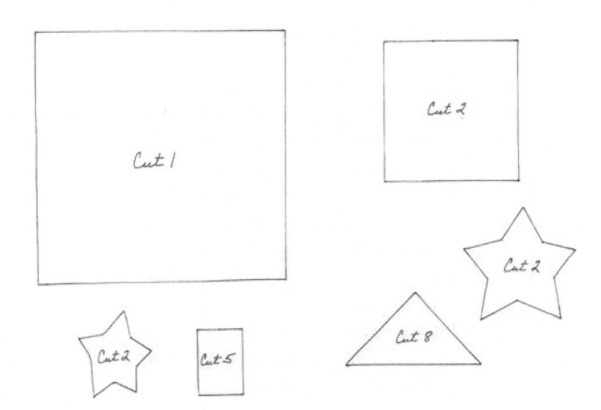

Cut 1

Cut 2

Cut 2

Cut 2

Cut 5

Cut 8

Dancing Stars Jumper

A penny saved is a penny to spend on fabric.

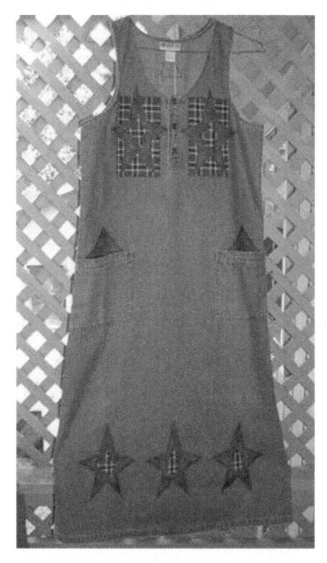

Print the full size applique patterns:

FreeApplique.com/applique.data/starpatt.jpg

FreeApplique.com/applique.data/hankiepatt1.jpg

FreeApplique.com/applique.data/hankiepatt2.jpg

Supplies:

Denim shirt
Fabric scraps

Thread to match
Fusible web

Dancing Stars Jumper Instructions

Follow the fusible web manufacturer's iron on instructions and iron the fusible web on the wrong side of the fabric.

From the fabric with the fusible web applied, cut two pieces 17 1/2" long by 1 1/4" wide. One will be for the collar and the other one will be used on a long sleeve shirt on the cuffs.

Trace the pattern pieces on the fusible web paper backing and cut out all pieces. Peel the fusible web paper backing from all pieces. Position each piece on shirt with right side of the fabric up. Iron pattern pieces on the shirt as directed for the fusible web.

Sew pieces on with a medium tight zigzag stitch.

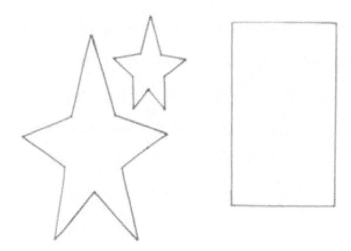

Hearts and Stars Shirt

Old seamstresses never go crazy, they just stay on pins and needles.

Print the full size applique patterns:
FreeApplique.com/applique.data/hstar1a.jpg

FreeApplique.com/applique.data/hstar2a.jpg

Supplies:

Denim shirt
Fabric scraps
Thread to match fabric
Fusible web

Hearts and Stars Shirt Instructions

Follow the fusible web manufacturer's iron on instructions and iron the fusible web on the wrong side of the fabric.

From the fabric with the fusible web applied, cut two pieces 17 1/2" long by 1 1/4" wide. One will be for the collar and the other one will be used on a long sleeve shirt on the cuffs.

Trace the pattern pieces on the fusible web paper backing and cut out all pieces. Peel the fusible web paper backing from all pieces. Position each piece on shirt with right side of the fabric up. Iron pattern pieces on the shirt as directed for the fusible web.

Sew pieces on with a medium tight zigzag stitch.

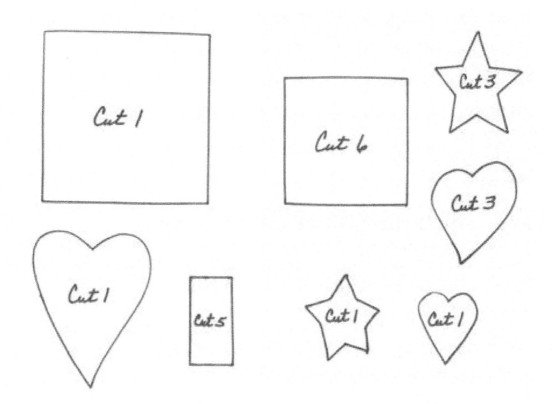

Cut 1

Cut 6

Cut 3

Cut 3

Cut 1

Cut 5

Cut 1

Cut 1

Patchwork Star

One yard of fabric, like one cookie, is never enough.

Print the full size applique patterns:
FreeApplique.com/applique.data/triangle.jpg

Supplies:

Denim shirt
Fabric scraps
Thread to match
Fusible web

Patchwork Star Shirt Instructions

Follow the fusible web manufacturer's iron on instructions and iron the fusible web on the wrong side of the fabric.

From the fabric with the fusible web applied, cut two pieces 17 1/2" long by 1 1/4" wide. One will be for the collar and the other one will be used on a long sleeve shirt on the cuffs.

Trace the pattern pieces on the fusible web paper backing and cut out all pieces. Peel the fusible web paper backing from all pieces. Position each piece on shirt with right side of the fabric up. Iron pattern pieces on the shirt as directed for the fusible web.

Sew pieces on with a medium tight zigzag stitch.

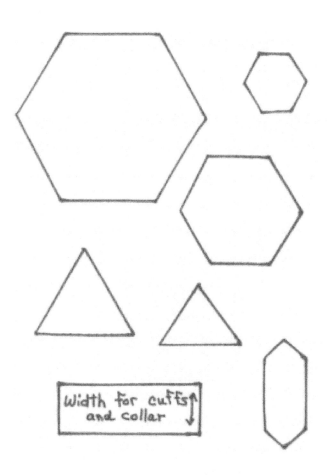

Width for cuffs
and collar ↑↓

117

Lone Star T-Shirt

I was Cut out to be RICH, but I was Sewed up WRONG.

Print the full size applique patterns:
FreeApplique.com/applique.data/lonestar1.gif
FreeApplique.com/applique.data/lonestar2.gif

Supplies:

T-Shirt
Fabric scraps
Thread to match fabric
Four small buttons
Fusible web

Lone Star T-Shirt Instructions

Follow the fusible web manufacturer's iron on instructions and iron the fusible web on the wrong side of the fabric.

Trace the pattern pieces on the fusible web paper backing and cut out all pieces. Peel the fusible web paper backing from all pieces. Position each piece on shirt with right side of the fabric up. Iron patterns on as directed for the fusible web.

Sew pieces on with a medium width loose zigzag stitch.

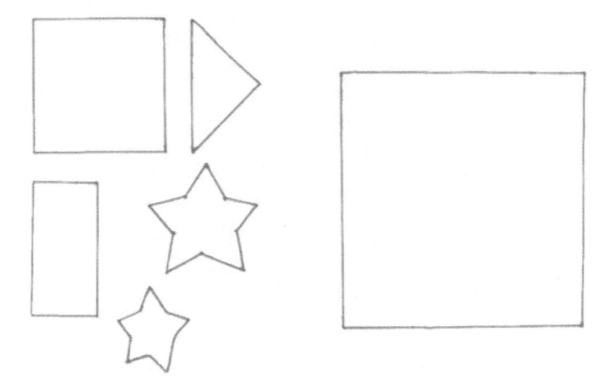

Panel Denim Shirt

Anytime is stitching time.

Print the full size applique patterns:
www.FreeApplique.com/applique.data/panel1a.gif
www.FreeApplique.com/applique.data/panel2d.gif
www.FreeApplique.com/applique.data/panel3.gif
www.FreeApplique.com/applique.data/panel4.gif
www.FreeApplique.com/applique.data/panel5.gif

Supplies:

Denim shirt
22" of fabric for panels and collar and cuffs
Thread to match
Fusible web

Panel Denim Shirt Instructions

The pattern for the panels is for a size large denim shirt. If you applique a larger shirt, you will have to add a little more all the way around the pattern.

First, pin the panels on both sides of the front of the shirt by turning under on all sides of the panel so you don't have any raw edges. Sew down with a loose zigzag stitch all the way around.

Then with fabric scraps to match the panels, you can add the hearts and stars. Iron fusible web to the fabric scraps. Follow the manufacturer's directions for ironing on the fusible web. With the panel fabric, you will make the collar and strip on the cuffs so you will have to iron the fusible web on that left over fabric too.

After you have the fusible web on the panel fabric, cut two strips 17 1/2" long by 1 1/4" wide. One strip will be for the collar and the other strip will go around the cuffs.

Trace the hearts and stars on the fabric scraps with the fusible web applied. Then cut all pieces and pull the fusible web paper backing off. Position each piece on the panels you had sewed on with right side up. Iron on pattern pieces on the panel as directed by fusible web. Sew the pattern pieces on with a medium tight zigzag.

This is a little harder to make and takes more time but it is well worth it.

MISCELLANEOUS PATTERNS

Here you'll find lots of fun ideas to add to your wardrobe and home. Horses, geometric designs, patchwork quilt patterns and flower shapes are just the start of a fun appliqué project.

Mix up the colors, prints and shapes to create memorable gift items and clothing. You can choose a theme or a color palette to get started. Then, the sky's the limit. There's no end to the combinations and ideas you'll come up with, once you get started.

Arkansas Block Shirt

Buttons and patches and the cold wind blowing
...the days pass quickly when I am sewing.

Print the full size applique patterns:
FreeApplique.com/applique.data/xpatt1.jpg
FreeApplique.com/applique.data/xpatt2.jpg

Supplies:

Denim shirt
Fabric scraps
Thread to match
Fusible web

Arkansas Block Shirt Instructions

Follow the fusible web manufacturer's iron on instructions and iron the fusible web on the wrong side of the fabric.

From the fabric with the fusible web applied, cut two pieces 17 1/2" long by 1 1/4" wide. One will be for the collar and the other one will be used on a long sleeve shirt on the cuffs.

Trace the pattern pieces on the fusible web paper backing and cut out all pieces. Peel the fusible web paper backing from all pieces. Position each piece on shirt with right side of the fabric up. Iron pattern pieces on the shirt as directed for the fusible web.

Sew pieces on with a medium tight zigzag stitch.

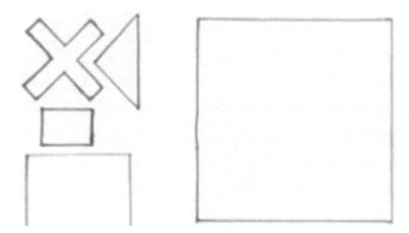

Arrow Applique Pattern

Behind every sewer is a huge pile of fabric. Use some of the fabric you've been collecting to make this sewing project.

Print the full size applique patterns:

FreeApplique.com/applique.data/arrow1a.jpg

FreeApplique.com/applique.data/arrow2a.jpg

Supplies:

Denim shirt
Fabric scraps
Thread to match fabric
Three small buttons
Fusible web

Arrow Shirt Instructions

Follow the fusible web manufacturer's iron on instructions and iron the fusible web on the wrong side of the fabric.

From the fabric with the fusible web applied, cut a piece 17 1/2" long and 1 1/4" wide. This will be the collar piece.

Trace the pattern pieces on the fusible web paper backing and cut out all pieces. Position each piece on shirt with right side of the fabric up. Iron patterns on as directed for the fusible web.

Sew pieces on with a medium width tight zigzag stitch. Or you can vary the stitch from tight to loose on different parts of the pattern pieces.

Sew a button on the top part of the heart. Sew two buttons on the square that is on the opposite side of the shirt.

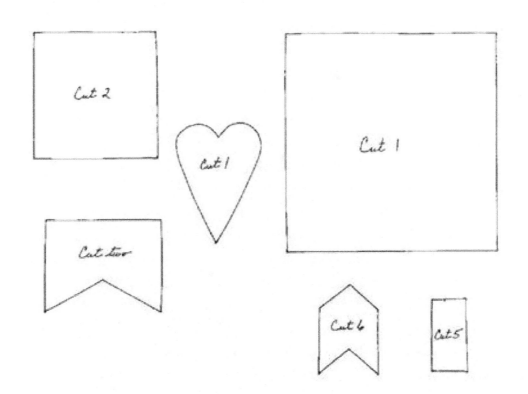

Autumn Harvest Shirt

Buttons & patches & cold wind blowing,
the days pass quickly when I'm sewing.

Print the full size applique patterns:
FreeApplique.com/applique.data/pumpkin1.gif
FreeApplique.com/applique.data/pumpkin2.gif

Supplies:

Fabric scraps in fall colors (Brown, tan, dark green and 3 different shades of orange)
Thread to match fabric
Fusible web

Autumn Harvest Instructions

Follow the fusible web manufacturer's iron on instructions and iron the fusible web on the wrong side of the fabric.

From the fabric with the fusible web applied, cut two pieces (out of orange) 17 1/2" long by 1 1/4" wide. One piece will be for the collar and the other one (cut in half to make 2 pieces: 8 3/4" by 1 1/4" each) will be used on the cuffs of a long sleeve shirt.

Trace the pattern pieces on the ironed on fusible web and cut out all pieces. Peel the fusible web paper backing from all pieces. Position each piece on the shirt with the right side of the fabric up. Iron the pattern pieces on the shirt as directed for the fusible web.

Sew pieces on with a medium tight zigzag stitch. When you are done sewing the pieces on, you are ready to start putting the lines on the pumpkin and the leaves. Use the same medium tight zigzag stitch for the lines.

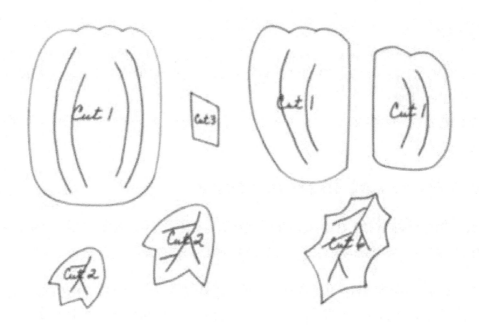

Cut 1

Cut 3

Cut 1

Cut 1

Cut 2

Cut 2

Cut 2

Basket Patch Shirt

Behind every sewer is a huge pile of fabric.
Make this basket patch denim shirt for the cool days ahead.

Print the full size applique patterns:
FreeApplique.com/applique.data/squarepat.jpg

Supplies:

Denim shirt
Fabric scraps
Thread to match
Fusible web

Basket Patch Shirt Instructions

Follow the fusible web manufacturer's iron on instructions and iron the fusible web on the wrong side of the fabric.

From the fabric with the fusible web applied, cut two pieces 17 1/2" long by 1 1/4" wide. One will be for the collar and the other one will be used on a long sleeve shirt on the cuffs.

Trace the pattern pieces on the fusible web paper backing and cut out all pieces. Peel the fusible web paper backing from all pieces. Position each piece on shirt with right side of the fabric up. Iron pattern pieces on the shirt as directed for the fusible web.

Sew pieces on with a medium tight zigzag stitch.

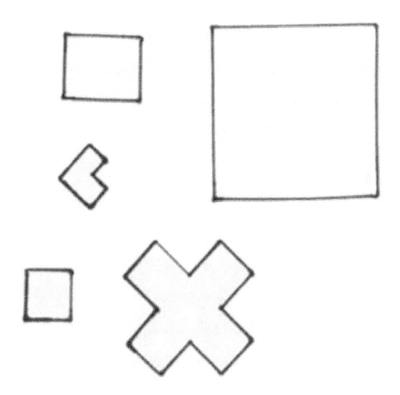

Clover T- Shirt

Anytime is stitching time....

Print the full size applique patterns:
FreeApplique.com/applique.data/childcloverpatt.gif

Supplies:

T-shirt
Fabric scraps
Thread to match
Fusible web

Clover T-shirt Instructions

Follow the fusible web manufacturer's iron on instructions and iron the fusible web on the wrong side of the fabric.

Trace the pattern pieces on the fusible web paper backing and cut out all pieces. Peel the fusible web paper backing from all pieces. Position each piece on the sweatshirt with right side of the fabric up. Iron pattern pieces on the sweatshirt as directed for the fusible web. Sew pieces on with a medium tight zigzag stitch.

Southwest Coyote Pattern

I cannot count my day complete
'Til needle, thread and fabric meet.

Print the full size applique patterns:
www.FreeApplique.com/Patterns/coyote1.html
www.FreeApplique.com/Patterns/coyote1a.html

Supplies:

Sweatshirt
Fabric scraps
Thread to match fabric
Fusible web

Southwest Coyote Sweatshirt Instructions

Follow the fusible web manufacturer's iron on instructions and iron the fusible web on the wrong side of the fabric.

Trace the pattern pieces on the fusible web paper backing and cut out all pieces. Peel the fusible web paper backing from all pieces. Position each piece on sweatshirt. Iron pattern pieces on the sweatshirt as directed for the fusible web.

Sew the pattern pieces on with a medium zigzag stitch.

Diamonds Applique Shirt

Print the full size applique patterns:
FreeApplique.com/applique.data/diamonds1.jpg
FreeApplique.com/applique.data/diamonds2.jpg

Supplies:

Denim shirt
Fabric scraps
Thread to match
Fusible web

Diamonds Applique Shirt Instructions

Follow the fusible web manufacturer's iron on instructions and iron the fusible web on the wrong side of the fabric.

From the fabric with the fusible web applied, cut two pieces 17 1/2" long by 1 1/4" wide. One will be for the collar and the other one will be used on a long sleeve shirt on the cuffs.

Trace the pattern pieces on the fusible web paper backing and cut out all pieces. Peel the fusible web paper backing from all pieces. Position each piece on shirt with right side of the fabric up. Iron pattern pieces on the shirt as directed for the fusible web.

Sew pieces on with a medium tight zigzag stitch.

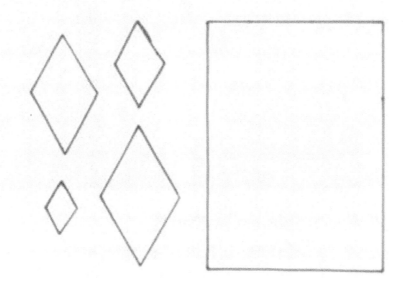

Flag T-Shirt Pattern

What better way to celebrate America than with this flag applique pattern.

Print the full size applique patterns:
FreeApplique.com/applique.data/flagpattern1.jpg

Supplies:

T-shirt

Fabric scraps
Thread to match fabric
Fusible web

Flag T-shirt Instructions

Follow the fusible web manufacturer's iron on instructions and iron the fusible web on the wrong side of the fabric.

Trace the pattern pieces on the fusible web paper backing and cut out all pieces. Position each piece on T-shirt with right side of the fabric up. Iron pattern pieces on as directed for the fusible web.

Sew pieces on with a medium width loose zigzag stitch.

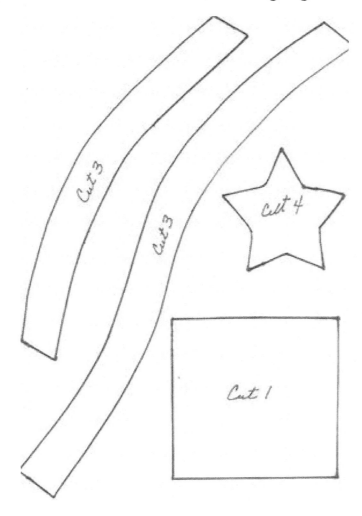

Golden Rod Shirt

I love sewing and have plenty of material witnesses.

Print the full size applique patterns:
www.FreeApplique.com/Patterns/goldenrod1.html
www.FreeApplique.com/Patterns/goldenrod3.html
www.FreeApplique.com/Patterns/goldenrod4.html

Supplies:

Denim shirt
Fabric scraps
Thread to match
Fusible web

Golden Rod Shirt Instructions

Follow the fusible web manufacturer's iron on instructions and iron the fusible web on the wrong side of the fabric.

From the fabric with the fusible web applied, cut two pieces 17 1/2" long by 1 1/4" wide. One will be for the collar and the other one will be used on a long sleeve shirt on the cuffs.

Trace the pattern pieces on the fusible web paper backing and cut out all pieces. Peel the fusible web paper backing from all pieces. Position each piece on shirt with right side of the fabric up. Iron pattern pieces on the shirt as directed for the fusible web.

Sew pieces on with a medium tight zigzag stitch.

Sew pieces on with a medium tight zigzag stitch.

Horse Sweatshirt Pattern

As you sew, so shall you rip.

Print the full size applique patterns:
www.FreeApplique.com/Patterns/horse1.html
www.FreeApplique.com/Patterns/horse1b.html

www.FreeApplique.com/Patterns/horse2.html
www.FreeApplique.com/Patterns/horse3.html
www.FreeApplique.com/Patterns/horse4.html
www.FreeApplique.com/Patterns/horse5.html

Supplies:

Sweatshirt
Fabric scraps
Thread to match fabric
Fusible web

Horse Sweatshirt Instructions

Iron fusible web to the wrong side of the fabric. Follow the manufacturer's directions for ironing on the fusible web.

Trace the pattern pieces on the fusible web paper backing and cut out all pieces. Peel the fusible web paper backing from all pieces. Position each piece on sweatshirt. Iron pattern pieces on the sweatshirt as directed for the fusible web.

Sew the pattern pieces on with a medium zigzag stitch.

Sew the pattern pieces on with a medium zigzag stitch.

Iceberg Sweatshirt Pattern

Stitch your stress away.

Print the full size applique patterns:

FreeApplique.com/applique.data/lavenderpatt1.jpg
FreeApplique.com/applique.data/lavenderpatt2.jpg

Supplies:

Sweatshirt
Fabric scraps
Thread to match fabric
Fusible web

Iceberg Sweatshirt Instructions

Follow the fusible web manufacturer's iron on instructions and iron the fusible web on the wrong side of the fabric.

Trace the pattern pieces on the fusible web paper backing and cut out all pieces. Peel the fusible web paper backing from all pieces. Position each piece on sweatshirt. Iron pattern pieces on the sweatshirt as directed for the fusible web.

Sew the pattern pieces on with a medium zigzag stitch.

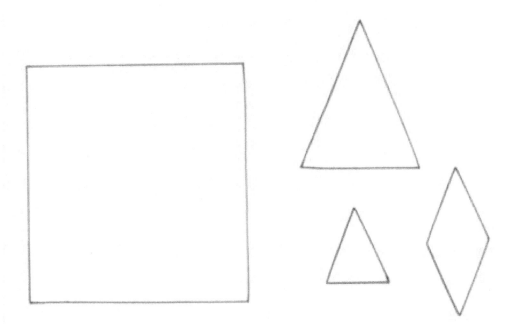

Pink and Teal Pattern

Print the full size applique patterns:

FreeApplique.com/applique.data/pinksspattern.jpg

Supplies:

Sweatshirt
Fabric scraps
Thread to match fabric
Fusible web
Purchased knit collar

Pink and Teal Sweatshirt Instructions

Follow the fusible web manufacturer's iron on instructions and iron the fusible web on the wrong side of the fabric.

Trace the pattern pieces on the fusible web paper backing and cut out all pieces. Peel the fusible web paper backing from all pieces. Position each piece on the sweatshirt. Iron the pattern pieces on the sweatshirt as in the directions for the fusible web.

Sew the pattern pieces on with a medium zigzag stitch.

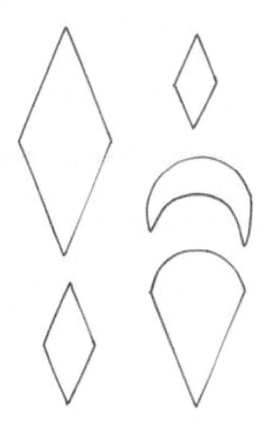

Pinwheel Sweatshirt Pattern

When life gives you scraps, make shirts!

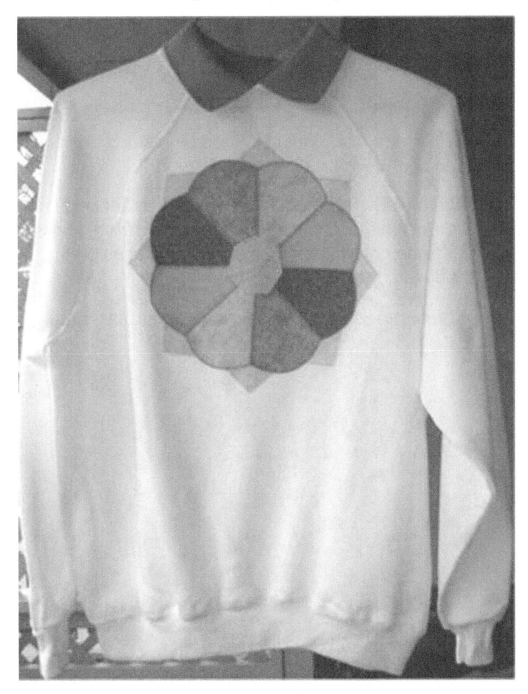

Print the full size applique patterns:
FreeApplique.com/applique.data/pinwheelss.gif

Supplies:

Sweatshirt
Fabric scraps
Thread to match fabric
Fusible web

Pinwheel Sweatshirt Instructions

Follow the fusible web manufacturer's iron on instructions and iron the fusible web on the wrong side of the fabric.

Trace the pattern pieces on the fusible web paper backing and cut out all pieces. Peel the fusible web paper backing from all pieces. Position each piece on sweatshirt. Iron pattern pieces on the sweatshirt as directed for the fusible web.

Sew the pattern pieces on with a medium zigzag stitch.

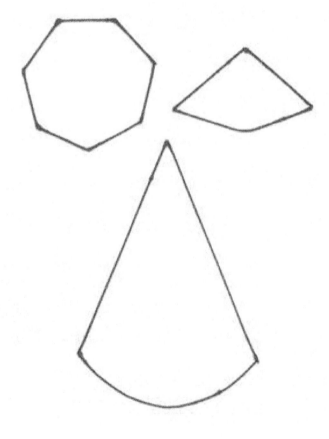

Preppie Applique Pattern

Print the full size applique patterns:

FreeApplique.com/applique.data/tanpattern1.jpg

FreeApplique.com/applique.data/tanpattern2.jpg

Supplies:

Sweatshirt
Fabric scraps
Thread to match fabric
Fusible web
Purchased knit collar

Preppie Sweatshirt Instructions

Follow the fusible web manufacturer's iron on instructions and iron the fusible web on the wrong side of the fabric.

Trace the pattern pieces on the fusible web paper backing and cut out all pieces. Peel the fusible web paper backing from all pieces. Position each piece on the sweatshirt. Iron the pattern pieces on the sweatshirt as in the directions for the fusible web.

Sew the pattern pieces on with a medium zigzag stitch.

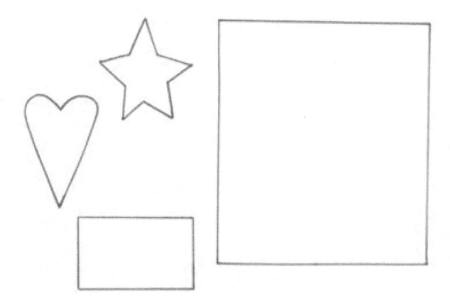

Southwestern Horse Pattern

A creative mess is better than tidy idleness.

Print the full size applique patterns:

FreeApplique.com/Patterns/southwesthorse1.html

FreeApplique.com/Patterns/southwesthorse2.html

Supplies:

Sweatshirt
Fabric scraps
Thread to match fabric
Fusible web

Southwest Sweatshirt Instructions

Follow the fusible web manufacturer's iron on instructions and iron the fusible web on the wrong side of the fabric.

Trace the pattern pieces on the fusible web paper backing and cut out all pieces. Peel the fusible web paper backing from all pieces. Position each piece on sweatshirt. Iron pattern pieces on the sweatshirt as directed for the fusible web. Sew the pattern pieces on with a medium zigzag stitch.

Triangle Cardigan Jacket

Never let a sewing machine know you are in a hurry....

Print the full size applique patterns:
FreeApplique.com/applique.data/triangle2a.gif

Supplies:

Cardigan sweatshirt
Fabric scraps
Thread to match
Fusible web

Triangle Cardigan Sweatshirt

Follow the fusible web manufacturer's iron on instructions and iron the fusible web on the wrong side of the fabric.

After doing the above, trace your pattern pieces on the fusible web and cut out all pieces. Remove fusible web paper backing from all pieces. Position each piece of sweatshirt with right side of the fabric up. Iron pattern pieces on the shirt as directed for the fusible web.

Sew pieces on with a medium tight zigzag stitch. I also added a few pieces of this design to the back of the sweatshirt.

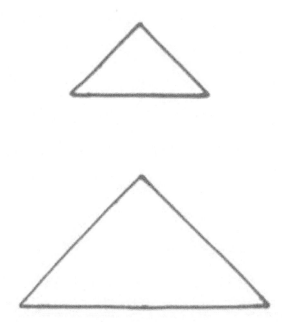

Windmill Sweatshirt Pattern

A fat quarter is not a body part!

Print the full size applique patterns:
www.FreeApplique.com/applique.data/windmill.gif

Supplies:

Sweatshirt
Fabric scraps
Thread to match fabric
Fusible web

Windmill Sweatshirt Instructions

Follow the fusible web manufacturer's iron on instructions and iron the fusible web on the wrong side of the fabric.

Trace the pattern pieces on the fusible web paper backing and cut out all pieces. Peel the fusible web paper backing from all pieces. Position each piece on sweatshirt. Iron pattern pieces on the sweatshirt as directed for the fusible web. Sew the pattern pieces on with a medium zigzag stitch.

Windmill Vest Pattern

Behind every sewer is a huge pile of fabric.

Photo shows front and back of vest

Print the full size applique patterns:

FreeApplique.com/applique.data/triangle1.gif

Supplies:

Vest
Fabric scraps
Thread to match
Fusible web

Windmill Vest Instructions

This is a very simple design to make and fun to sew. You can put this design on any vest. I also added the design to the back as you can see in the picture.

Follow the fusible web manufacturer's iron on instructions and iron the fusible web on the wrong side of the fabric.

Trace the pattern pieces on the fusible web paper backing and cut out all pieces. Peel the fusible web paper backing from all pieces. Position each piece on shirt with right side of the fabric up. Iron pattern pieces on the vest with right side of the fabric up. Iron pattern pieces on the vest as directed for the fusible web.

Sew pieces on with a tight zigzag stitch.

CHILDREN'S PATTERNS

Kids love color, and appliqués are a quick and easy way to add punch to shirts, skirts, pants and accessories for a child's room. Teddy bears, puppies and kittens make great embellishments, and you can use any color or combination to create cute and practical items for your child to wear and enjoy.

Child's Clover Sweatshirt

Sewing and crafts fill my days....Not to mention the living room, bedroom and closet.

Print the full size applique patterns:

FreeApplique.com/Patterns/childcloverpat.html

Supplies:

Child's sweatshirt
Fabric scraps
Thread to match
Fusible web

Child's Clover Sweatshirt Instructions

Follow the fusible web manufacturer's iron on instructions and iron the fusible web on the wrong side of the fabric.

Trace the pattern pieces on the fusible web paper backing and cut out all pieces. Peel the fusible web paper backing from all pieces. Position each piece on sweatshirt with right side of the fabric up. Iron pattern pieces on the sweatshirt as directed for the fusible web. Sew pieces on with a medium tight zigzag stitch.

Child's Kitty Sweatshirt

Sewing mends the soul.

Print the full size applique patterns:
FreeApplique.com/Patterns/childkittypat.html

Supplies:

Child's Sweatshirt or T-Shirt
Fabric scraps
Thread to match
Fusible web
Small amount of ribbon

Child's Kitty Sweatshirt Instructions

Follow the fusible web manufacturer's iron on instructions and iron the fusible web on the wrong side of the fabric.

Trace the pattern pieces on the fusible web paper backing and cut out all pieces. Peel the fusible web paper backing from all pieces. Position each piece on sweatshirt or T-Shirt with right side of the fabric up. Iron pattern pieces on the shirt as directed for the fusible web.

Sew pieces on with a medium tight zigzag stitch.

Child's Puppy Sweatshirt

My husband lets me buy all the fabric I can hide.

Print the full size applique patterns:
FreeApplique.com/Patterns/childpuppypat.html

Supplies:

Child's Sweatshirt or T-Shirt
Fabric scraps
Thread to match
Fusible web
Small amount of ribbon

Child's Puppy Sweatshirt Instructions

Follow the fusible web manufacturer's iron on instructions and iron the fusible web on the wrong side of the fabric.

Trace the pattern pieces on the fusible web paper backing and cut out all pieces. Peel the fusible web paper backing from all pieces. Position each piece on sweatshirt or T-Shirt with right side of the fabric up. Iron pattern pieces on the shirt as directed for the fusible web.

Sew pieces on with a medium tight zigzag stitch.

Child's Teddy Bear Sweatshirt

May your bobbin always be full.

Print the full size applique patterns:

FreeApplique.com/Patterns/childteddybearpat.html

Supplies:

Child's Sweatshirt or T-Shirt
Fabric scraps
Thread to match
Fusible web
Small amount of ribbon

Teddy Bear Sweatshirt Instructions

Follow the fusible web manufacturer's iron on instructions and iron the fusible web on the wrong side of the fabric.

Trace the pattern pieces on the fusible web paper backing and cut out all pieces. Peel the fusible web paper backing from all pieces. Position each piece on sweatshirt or T-Shirt with right side of the fabric up. Iron pattern pieces on the shirt as directed for the fusible web. Sew pieces on with a medium tight zigzag stitch.

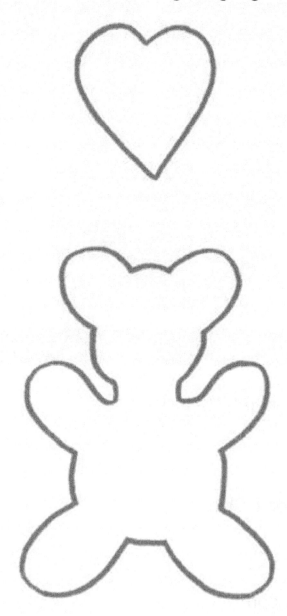

Photo credits:
Cover photo by Daria Karaulnik/Photos.com

Other photos and backgrounds:
Olga Telnova
Tatiananna
Crystal67
Neeley Spotts
Marina Glazova
Olga Usikova

Printed in Great Britain
by Amazon

40730564R00099